I0617570

A STORY OF
BRAINS
AND
BELLIES
AN INTRODUCTION TO EMETOPHOBIA

AMY VANTE

The phrase "throwing up" is used exclusively throughout this book in order to minimize potentially triggering language.

The content of this book is for informational purposes only and does not substitute professional medical advice or consultations with healthcare professionals.

Copyright © 2023 Amy Vante
All Rights Reserved. No parts of this book may be reproduced in any form without permission from the author or publisher, except as permitted by U.S. copyright law. Edition I. Cedar Rapids, Iowa, USA
ISBN 9798989213603
Published by Amethyst Books 2023
Library of Congress Control Number: 2023919130

AB

Table of Contents

Preface

It's been said that a worried mom does better research than the FBI, and my investigation into emetophobia has proven no exception.

When one of my children developed an intense fear of throwing up, it became my mission to learn as much as I could about this often misunderstood and underrecognized condition.

Let me assure you - my lifelong aspirations never included authoring a book about throwing up! It was only after the challenging process of learning about and finding ways to explain emetophobia to others that I decided to create a resource meant to simplify that information and help spread awareness of it.

For those of us who care about someone with emetophobia, the importance of validation to those experiencing it can't be understated. I wish I had known sooner that simply allowing fears to be expressed and acknowledged without shame or dispute could be so beneficial.

Understanding emetophobia is an important step in dealing with its unique challenges.

The primal need for safety is stronger than willpower. An emetophobic person's fear is an expression of their body doing precisely what it was designed to do - to keep them safe.

To recognize this can be liberating.

Part 1

The Body

There are many different organs and systems inside your body. While they each have jobs of their own, they also work together as a team to keep you safe and healthy.

Two organs that work especially well together are...

THE STOMACH + THE BRAIN

Your brain and stomach are like best friends. They are always in contact with each other and have a lot in common. One of the traits they share is that a lot of the work they accomplish happens without you thinking about it.

By communicating through **neurons** in your body's **autonomic nervous system**, organs like your brain and stomach are able to do many things without your awareness.

When your body does something without conscious effort, it is called an **involuntary action.** Breathing, blinking, and swallowing are a few examples of involuntary actions.

Part 2

The Brain

The brain is your body's control system. It uses nerves to send and receive messages throughout your body.

Your actions and behaviors are all regulated by your brain, so it has a really big workload! It is in charge of making sure involuntary actions get done, along with many other important things like storing memories, processing emotions, and interpreting any information it receives from your senses. *Your brain's most important job is to make sure you stay safe.*

To keep you out of harm's way, your brain remains on constant lookout for signs of any potential danger. It never stops gathering information about your surroundings in order to check for threats that might be nearby. It does all of this automatically, and most of the time you are unaware of it.

If your brain does detect a threat, it will make sure the rest of your body knows about it right away.

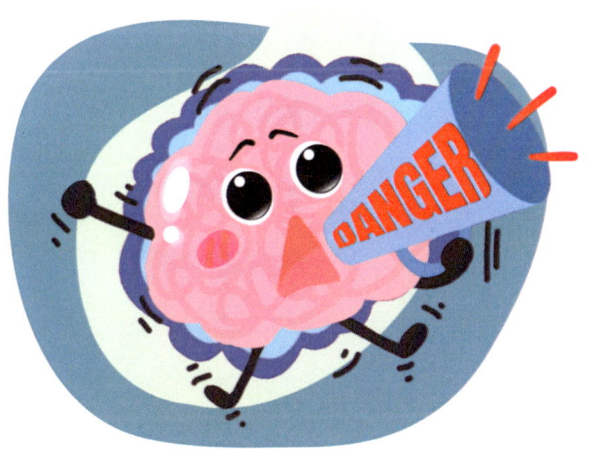

The area of your brain that alerts the rest of your body to danger doesn't use language. Instead, it uses thoughts and feelings to communicate.

In order to detect danger, your brain first has to decide what is dangerous and what is not. The **genes** you were born with and the experiences you have in life provide the information your brain uses to make this decision.

It's common for people to fear different things because everyone has a different mix of genes and experiences.

Any time your brain categorizes something as dangerous, you will fear that thing. Fear is the **emotional response** that happens when danger is detected.

Occasionally, your brain is unsure if something is dangerous or not. When this happens, your brain still has to make a decision about safety.

Since your brain takes every precaution when it comes to safety, it categorizes anything it feels uncertain about as threatening.

Being cautious is great for survival, but this means that your brain might occasionally decide something poses a threat even though it isn't really dangerous.

Part 3

The Stomach

Your stomach also does a lot to keep you safe and healthy. For example, it stores and breaks down food. Many people are surprised to learn that it also plays a role in regulating emotions.

Part of your nervous system is housed inside the lining of your stomach. This means that there are many nerves in your stomach, all capable of gathering information.

These nerves send and receive messages with your brain about everything they sense. This means your thoughts are able to affect how your stomach feels and vice versa.

Nerves like the ones in the lining of your stomach are able to exchange their information back and forth with the brain very quickly - in only a small fraction of a second.

Having part of your nervous system located in your stomach also makes it possible to experience feelings there, like the "knots" or "butterflies" you may feel when you get nervous.

Your stomach's nerves detect a lot of things. They can tell how full or empty your stomach is and even sense when something harmful has entered your stomach.

When something unhealthy (like a germ or bad food) enters your stomach, the muscles surrounding your stomach squeeze hard to push the unwanted contents back up and out of your body. This process is sometimes called throwing up.

Part 4

Emetophobia

Emetophobia *is the intense fear of throwing up.*

Most people don't like throwing up and find it to be unpleasant, but an emetophobic person's reaction to it is much more intense.

In spite of their best efforts, they can't stop worrying about throwing up. It's the last thing they want to think about, but it stays on their mind a lot. The fear they feel is genuine, even though their worries might not make sense to others. *Their response to throwing up is atypical because their brain believes throwing up is a threat to their personal safety.*

People with emetophobia might feel confused, embarrassed, or ashamed about the way they react to throwing up. They may not understand why they respond differently than others do or why they can't stop worrying about something they'd rather not even think about.

Emetophobic people wish their worries and fears didn't happen.

In spite of this, the unwanted fears and worries keep showing up... and they often appear unexpectedly.

An emetophobic person's brain reacts to throwing up very differently than the brain of someone who doesn't have emetophobia.

Unlike other brains, the brains of emetophobic people have categorized throwing up as:

When an emetophobic person's brain feels threatened by throwing up, it starts the process of alerting the rest of the body to its distress.

Nervousness, anxiety, and stomach discomfort are ways the body might respond to these distress signals. Stomach discomfort and unusual sensations like these often remind emetophobic people of throwing up. When this happens, the stomach creates its own distress signal to send back to the brain.

This is where the problem begins.

The cycle of distress between the brain and the stomach can go on and on until total panic and fear take over.

This process can cause an emetophobic person's entire body to respond as though they are in extreme danger.

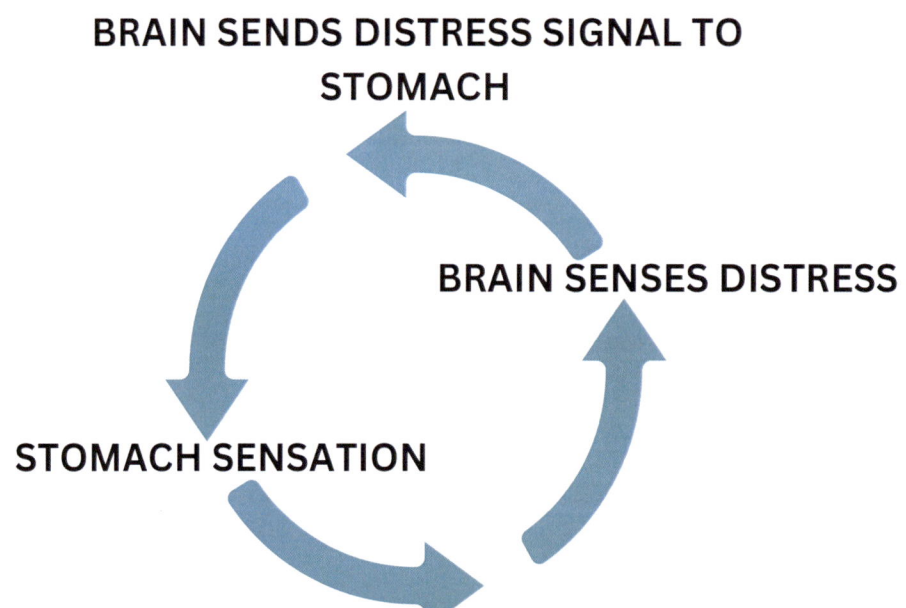

BRAIN SENDS DISTRESS SIGNAL TO STOMACH

BRAIN SENSES DISTRESS

STOMACH SENSATION

STOMACH SENDS DISTRESS SIGNAL TO BRAIN

If you think you might have emetophobia, read on to learn more about it and how you can begin to overcome your fear of throwing up.

Part 5

Understanding Emetophobia

Emetophobic worries vary from person to person. For example, some people worry mostly about themselves throwing up while others worry more about someone else throwing up around them.

No one knows for sure what causes emetophobia. A lot of people who have emetophobia have other types of anxiety, too (especially **OCD**). Traumatic experiences involving throwing up could play a role in developing this phobia.

Once the brain has categorized throwing up as dangerous, emetophobic behavior occurs as a fear response to that danger.

Your **amygdala** is one of two almond-shaped structures deep inside your brain. It is the part of your brain in charge of identifying threats and signaling a stress response if one is present.

Your amygdala can act independently of the other areas in your brain. This means the amygdala can perceive something as a threat in spite of the rest of your brain knowing the threat isn't real.

When a threat is detected, your amygdala's alert signals travel quickly throughout the brain and nervous system to prepare your entire body to face danger.

Three of the most common survival tactics that your body could use to keep you safe are **fight**, **flight**, and **freeze**.

Tactics like these influence your behavior until you feel safe again.

When you experience the intense fear caused by emetophobia, you probably act differently than you normally would. This happens because the amygdala's fear response inside your brain has taken control.

When released, its distress signals overtake the ability to think logically in other areas of your brain.

You might have a hard time thinking rationally or even speaking when this happens due to all of the changes taking place inside your brain.

This can make it especially difficult to explain to others what you are going through.

Scanning the environment for threats is another involuntary action your brain engages in. When a threat is detected, you might begin to feel worried about throwing up without knowing exactly why.

This happens because the part of your brain in charge of finding threats cannot use language to communicate its findings. Instead, it uses feelings.

The places, words, and even thoughts your brain associates with a threat become part of the clues your brain looks out for. These clues are also called **triggers**.

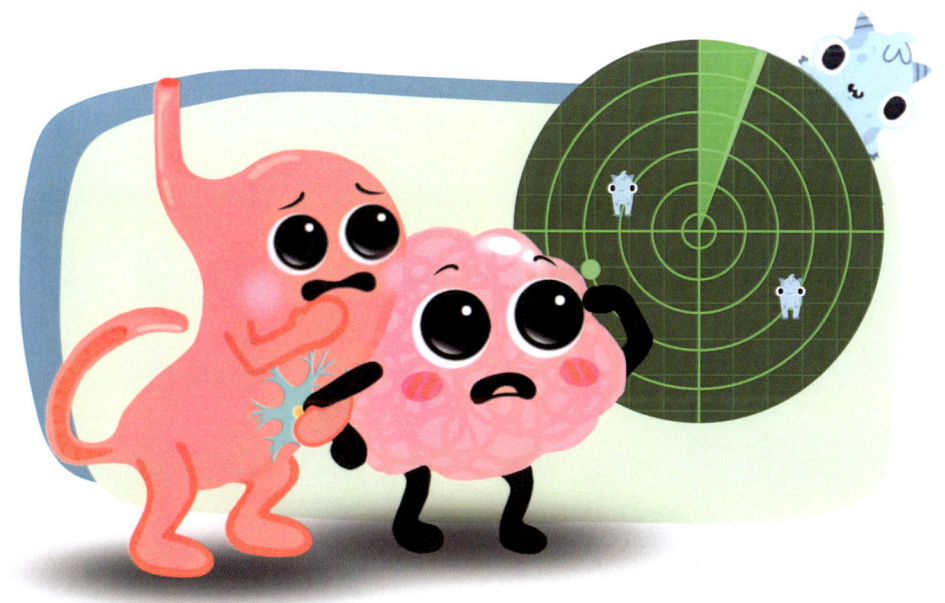

Since your brain wants to keep you safe, it gives you feelings that make you want to avoid triggers. In an effort to avoid them, you might develop certain behaviors to help you feel safe. These are called **safety behaviors**.

For example, if you are at school and someone throws up, your brain might start to associate school with throwing up. Refusing to go to school or avoiding the person who threw up are examples of safety behaviors that could develop in response to this scenario.

Here are more examples of safety behaviors emetophobic people might use:

- *Smelling food before eating it*
- *Checking expiration dates on food excessively*
- *Taking unnecessary medicine*
- *Retreating to or refusing to leave a place where you feel safe*
- *Staying near a person who gives you comfort*
- *Chewing gum often*
- *Keeping a bag or bowl nearby*
- *Avoiding people, places, or things that remind you of throwing up*
- *Refusing transportation that could cause motion sickness*
- *Declining medical care involving the throat, mouth, or stomach*
- *Refusing to wear clothes that were worn during emetophobic experiences*

- Restricting foods or refusing to eat
- Staying away from alcohol and drinking
- Avoiding amusement parks or motion rides at playgrounds
- Avoiding crowds and babies
- Cleaning things excessively, including surroundings, clothes, and body
- Refusing to use public bathrooms or touch door handles
- Discarding clothing, toys, or other objects associated with throwing up
- Compulsively sharing worries and concerns
- Avoiding language and discussions that involve throwing up
- Avoiding anyone who may be sick

Safety behaviors are supposed to make you feel better, but they end up doing the opposite. Safety behaviors actually perpetuate the distress - and can even make it worse.

The problem with safety behaviors is that they reinforce the fear of throwing up.

Each time you perform a safety behavior, you are agreeing with your brain that throwing up is dangerous. When you repeatedly agree with your brain that something is dangerous and should be avoided, your brain works even harder to avoid that thing.

**BRAIN BELIEVES
TRIGGER IS DANGEROUS**

**SAFETY BEHAVIOR PERFORMED
TO AVOID TRIGGER**

As a result, your brain increases its sensitivity to emetophobic danger. This is why safety behaviors actually make you worry *more* about throwing up.

Part
6

Overcoming Emetophobia

Emetophobia can limit your ability to enjoy life to the fullest. For some people, it can even be debilitating. The good news is that in the same way your brain learned to fear throwing up, it can also learn to tolerate it.

To lessen the effects of emetophobia, you will need to teach your brain that throwing up is NOT dangerous. There are several ways to do this, and you can choose the one that feels right for you.

Talking to a professional counselor or therapist about emetophobia allows you to work through fears in a safe environment. You might learn things like how to stay calm when you are anxious or how to challenge the negative thoughts you have about throwing up. There are many ways to get this type of support.

Cognitive Behavioral Therapy (CBT)

CBT is a form of therapy that helps to change behaviors by talking about them. During CBT, a trained professional listens to your problems and asks you questions about them. They will help you understand your thought processes and problem solve with you to create ideas for changing the negative ways you think and feel. Usually, CBT is done in sessions of 30 to 60 minutes and continues on a weekly or semi-weekly basis for as long as you need it.

Eye Movement Desensitization and Reprocessing (EMDR)

EMDR involves a trained professional working with you to encourage your brain to store your fears in a less reactive part of your brain. When this happens, it helps to calm the responses you have to those thoughts. During EMDR, the therapist guides you through simple movements (oftentimes just moving your eyes) in order to activate different areas of your brain while you think about and discuss your emetophobia. EMDR usually takes about an hour per session and can be done as many times as it takes to overcome your phobia. Some people respond quickly to EMDR while others might require more sessions.

Exposure Therapy

Exposure therapy is a very effective way of overcoming phobias. It involves taking small steps towards overcoming your fears one at a time.

During exposure therapy, behaviors you'd like to overcome are written down in order of least distressing to most distressing. This list is called a **hierarchy of fear,** and it helps guide the steps that will be taken during exposure therapy.

Beginning with the least distressing fear on your list and then working up to more challenging fears, each fear is faced in a controlled way. If at any time the next step feels too distressing, you can just keep practicing the step you are on.

As you experience each new fear, your brain becomes less afraid. Your bravery teaches your brain that throwing up is not dangerous after all.

Since finding appropriate ways to expose yourself to fear might require encouragement and creativity, it can be helpful to work with a professional when doing exposure therapy. Alternatively, you can work through it on your own or with the help of a supportive friend or family member.

Hypnotherapy

Guided hypnosis performed by a trained hypnotherapist can influence the areas of your brain where subconscious thoughts and fears take place. During hypnosis, you feel focused and relaxed as you explore a guided thought process. Examining your phobia in this altered state of mind can change the way your brain perceives and responds to it. Hypnotherapy sessions vary in duration and can be repeated as needed. For treatment of phobias, multiple sessions are typically recommended.

Practice and patience are especially important during any type of therapy. It's normal to have setbacks and it's okay to take as much time as you need to feel comfortable.

You might choose to meet with a few different professionals in order to find one that's just right for you. Many therapy services are also available online, which means you can meet with a therapist from home if you prefer. If you attend school, school counselors can offer support to you there as well.

Now that you know more about emetophobia, you can decide what method might serve you best in overcoming your fears. By setting goals for yourself and working towards positive change, you can teach your brain and belly to accept throwing up as a natural process that is designed to keep the body safe from harm.

Learning more about your fears reduces the power they have over you. By reading this book, you've already taken a great step forward in overcoming emetophobia!

A Note to Caretakers

Witnessing the struggles of someone you love can be distressing and it might be difficult to know how you can help. Here are a few ways you can offer support to a person with emetophobia:

- Acknowledge that their fear is genuine, even if it is illogical or confusing.
- Allow them to experience their fear in a safe environment. The more they resist it, the more ingrained it becomes.
- Do your best to remain calm and present during emetophobic attacks.
- Talk to them about their emetophobia during low-stress times and ask if there are specific ways you can offer support.
- Communicate with teachers, counselors, and medical professionals in order to advocate for an emetophobic child.
- Seek support for yourself if you become overwhelmed or need guidance.
- Finding a therapist or doctor who has experience specifically in treating phobias is particularly helpful.

Glossary

Amygdala
Part of the brain associated with fear, emotion, and motivation.

Autonomic Nervous System
The part of the body's nervous system that is in charge of functions that happen automatically.

Digestive System
The parts of the body that work together to turn food and liquids into fuel.

Emetophobia
An intense and seemingly irrational fear of throwing up.

Emotional Response
Reactive feelings and behaviors.

Fight, Flight, and Freeze
Aggression, running away, or holding still in response to danger.

Genes
Found inside the DNA of cells, these are responsible for inherited traits.

Hierarchy of fear
A list of concerns, ranked from the least fearful to the most fearful.
Involuntary Actions
Acts performed by the body that the mind doesn't have conscious control over.
Neurons
Nerve cells found throughout the body that carry messages to and from the brain.
Nervous System
Includes the nerves, brain, and spinal cord; a communication network within the body.
Obsessive Compulsive Disorder (OCD)
Anxiety disorder involving disruptive or out-of-control thoughts.
Safety Behaviors
Actions meant to prevent fear or to feel more comfortable.
Triggers
Anything that causes an emotional reaction.

Safety Behaviors

○ ....

○ ....

○ ....

○ ....

○ ....

○ ....

Triggers

○ ....

○ ....

○ ....

○ ....

○ ....

○ ....

Hierarchy of Fear

Level of Distress Experienced

www.ingramcontent.com/pod-product-compliance
Lightning Source LLC
Chambersburg PA
CBRC090839120626
46551CB00008B/708